JUN 2 6 2006

MEL BAY PRESENTS

DRUMMIN
FACTS, TIPS & WARM-UPS

BY MAT MARUCCI

Recorded at Blue Crystal Studios, Jeff Bond: Engineer. Produced by Mat Marucci.
Cover photo courtesy of Mapex USA, Inc.

Visit us on the Web at www.melbay.com – E-mail us at email@melbay.com

MEL BAY
QWIKGUIDE®

CONTENTS

FOREWORD

In my years of teaching and playing professionally, there have been a variety of questions that I have been asked by students and other drummers. These include subjects such as tuning or tensioning the drums, achieving certain sounds from them, the differences in drumheads, drumsticks and cymbals, practicing techniques and routines, keeping good time and a steady groove, playing a smooth roll, practicing the drum rudiments and exercises to improve certain aspects of their playing.

This book addresses all of those subjects in an informative way by having whole chapters that focus on the different drumming facts, tips and information that most drummers need to know and need to learn somewhere.

This book culminates with a routine that can either be used as a warm-up that will take approximately 15 minutes or can be developed into a longer practice session and become a real "chops builder". Whatever the reader's level of drumming, I'm sure this book will have something of interest for everyone.

CHAPTER 1

BASIC POINTS

1) <u>The Fulcrum:</u> Your grip of the stick begins and ends with the fulcrum. This should be at a point on the stick I call the comfortable or practical balance point - a point where the stick is not perfectly balanced but slightly top heavy so the bead of the stick will fall toward the drum and the stick will move and rebound freely. For the matched grip fulcrum, the stick should be pinched between the thumb and first joint of the index (1st) finger. For traditional grip the stick should be squeezed in the crook between the thumb and the index finger. The rest of the fingers in both grips should be wrapped lightly around the stick to control and manipulate the strokes and rebounds.

Common mistakes:

a) Holding the sticks too far back behind the practical balance point making the stick too top heavy. This prevents the stick from rebounding freely after stroking the drum.

b) Gripping the stick with the fingers instead of just at the fulcrum point. This not only inhibits the stick rebound but also finger manipulation of the stick. If you are using the fingers to hold the stick you can not use them for other movements.

c) Closing the gap between the thumb and index finger using the matched grip. There should be an oval shaped space between them and they should not touch each other - touching only the stick at the fulcrum.

d) Taking the index finger off and away from the stick with the traditional grip. There can be a space between finger and the stick but the finger should always remain <u>over</u> the stick. The finger cannot be used if it is not in position over the stick.

2) <u>Stick Position:</u> The percussion family has the only instruments with which the player does not have direct contact. Instead, certain instruments use an intermediary such as drumsticks, mallets and brushes. Because of this fact it is essential that the stick becomes an extension of the arm and hand of the drummer.

To help accomplish this, the stick in the matched grip hand should be in the center of the palm. When holding the stick there is a groove in the center of the palm that almost seems it was made for a drumstick. When in the center the stick looks like a true extension of the arm.

In the traditional grip hand the stick should be at an angle that if the fingers were opened and pointed towards the center of the drum the stick would almost look like one extra finger on the inside of the hand.

Common errors:
   a) Holding the matched grip stick at an angle to the hand with the butt end extending from the side. In addition to not being a true extension of the arm and hand this also forces the player to hold onto the stick with the fingers instead of just at the fulcrum. Again, if the fingers are holding the stick they cannot manipulate it as efficiently.

   b) Holding the traditional grip at too sharp an angle. This is usually caused by keeping the hand more in the closed than open position. None of the fingers should touch the palm of the hand. When the hand is more open the stick moves and rebounds more freely - and the fingers are more relaxed and better able to manipulate the stick.

3) <u>Hand Position:</u> This is the number one problem I have found with students - from beginner to advanced. If the hand position is wrong then the fulcrum cannot be used effectively which prevents the stick from moving freely, which inhibits the rebound, etc., etc., etc. Matched grip has two <u>basic</u> positions: palm down, knuckles up; and thumb up. The classic traditional grip has the hand in the position as if holding a glass of water. There should be no bend at the wrist with either grip - just a straight line from the forearm down to the knuckles.

4) <u>Sticking:</u> Generally, but with exceptions, when doing hand-to-hand techniques keeping mind the phrase "one stick up, one stick down". When using this system you will always have a stick in position to make a stroke from either the high ("up") position of low ("down") position. "For every action there is an equal and opposite reaction" -Physics axiom. (Example: When one stick is moving toward the drum from the high position, the other stick should be moving to the high position at the same time - passing each other at mid-stroke.) This system keeps the hands feeling balanced.

5) <u>Stick Height:</u> This is different from sticking in that it refers to how high you bring the sticks. Whether you work from a full 90 degree position, a 45 degree angle or anything else in between, the important point is that both sticks return to the same height. Because most of us are not ambidextrous we have a tendency to favor our strong hand and bring that stick to a higher position than the weak hand. This means one stick is traveling a shorter distance to reach the drum whenever a stroke is made. It stands to reason that if one stick is traveling eight inches and the other only five inches, the stick farther away has to move faster to reach the drum in the same time interval as the closer stick. This also means the rebound will be weaker with the closer stick.

6) <u>Playing Off The Drum:</u> Unless they have learned this somewhere along the way, most drummers, especially heavy hitters, play down into the drum instead of off it. When making your stroke think "up" and bring the stick away from the head immediately after striking it. Some teachers describe this as "drawing" or "pulling" the sound out of the drum. The shorter the time the stick is on the drumhead the more resonant and responsive the drum will be. Thus, a cleaner and fuller tone and increased stick speed.

7) <u>Playing Off Center:</u> That a drum should be played dead center is a fallacy. The center is the weakest and deadest part of the drum head. This means less response, less tone and less rebound. In addition, a drum head will break easiest when hit in the center.

Both sticks cannot play efficiently in the same spot without getting in each other's way. "Two objects cannot occupy the same space at the same time" -Physics axiom. The right stick should be played to the right center and the left stick to the left center. The distance from the center depends on the situation. The closer to the center, the less ring - the closer to the rim, the more sensitivity and response.

All of the previous basics should be concentrated on during practice sessions until they are second nature to the drummer. But when at a rehearsal or job the concentration should be totally on the music - and playing musically.

CHAPTER 2

TUNING THE DRUM

There are those who say that "tuning" is an improper term in reference to a drum unless a definite pitch is attained such as with a timpani. The drum is actually "tensioned" rather than "tuned". However, since the drum should be in tune with itself, the term "tune" is still valid even when applied to a drum without definite pitch.

There are three ways to tune any drum: 1) the top (batter) head tighter than the bottom head; 2) the bottom head tighter than the batter head; and 3) both heads the same tension. There is also a process called "de-tuning".

Tuning Effects:

1) Batter Head Tighter: This tensioning tends to emphasize the mid to low tones of the drum and creates a slow decay of the sound - which means the heads vibrate for a longer time and the tone sustains with more overtones than other tunings.

2) Bottom Head Tighter: This tensioning tends to emphasize the mid to high tones of the drum and creates a quicker decay than other tunings - short sustain, less overtones.

3) Both Heads Equal: This creates a full, round sound with a medium decay and a tone almost an exact note. Tuning to a particular note should be avoided if it lies within the harmonic structure of other instruments or diatonic scales because the note produced by the drum could clash with an instrument playing in certain key signatures.

4) De-tuning: This creates the effect of a slow or slight bend to the tone produced by the head that is de-tuned.

Snare Drum Effects:

1) Batter Head Tighter - Full, snarry, warm sound

2) Snare Head Tighter - Tight, sharp sound; fast decay

Important: Each size drum has its own particular tuning range and each size drum will sound its best when tensioned within that range. A large drum should not be over-tensioned to achieve a high sound and conversely, a small drum should not be tensioned too loosely to obtain a deep sound. If the pitch does not lie comfortably in the drum's range, a smaller or larger drum is needed.

THE TUNING PROCESS

Whatever combination of head tension is chosen by the drummer, the most important step is to make sure the drum and each head is in tune with itself. This means that the tension is the same at each tension rod so that by tapping the drum the same distance from each (approximately 1" - 2") it produces the same tone.

Once the head is on the shell and the hoops or rims are in place over it the tensioning may be done clockwise, counterclockwise or cross-tensioning.

Examples:

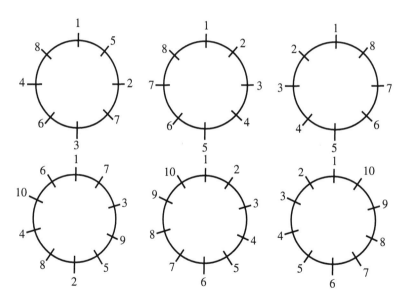

Clockwise tensioning would be in the order 1-2-3-4-5-6-7-8. Counterclockwise would be 1-8-7-6-5-4-3-2. And cross-tensioning would be 1-5-3-7-2-6-4-8. (Cross-tensioning is the preferred method - especially for fine tuning.)

Start the tuning process gradually, doing each tension rod three or four times to get the wrinkles out of the head and to get the head tight enough to produce a tone. At this point, press the palm of one hand in the center of the drumhead and push down firmly. Cracks and pops will be heard, especially on coated plastic heads, as the head material stretches and the head is "seated" evenly on the shell. Repeat the tensioning process again as the seating of the head will release some tension from the previous tightening. Now, repeat the seating process again.

When the drumhead is at the desired tension <u>after</u> the final seating, it is time to fine tune it. Tap the head at the same distance from each tension rod as described earlier and tighten or loosen each one until they are all producing the same tone.

Helpful hint: Place your index finger very lightly in the center of the head while fine tuning as this will eliminate many of the overtones and make the <u>primary</u> tone the head is producing easier to hear.

Important: As noted earlier, each drum size has its own range and should be tuned comfortably within that range to achieve the best sound.

CHAPTER 3

DRUMHEADS

Drumheads were originally made with the actual skins of animals. These heads gave a very warm sound to the drum but also had considerable problems with consistency, stretching and being affected by weather. Humidity in particular wreaked havoc with calfskin heads. It was necessary to re-tension the drum each time it was played after being stored. In fact, the calfskin heads were actually loosened when the drum was stored to prevent stretching of the head due to heat.

With the creation of plastic drumheads, the vast majority of the problems with calfskin heads were eliminated. Nowadays, while it is still possible to purchase real calfskin heads from specialty suppliers, the vast majority of drummers use the modern plastic drumheads that were developed in the 1950s. These plastic heads virtually eliminated the problems that were associated with heads made of real calfskin.

Today's plastic heads have evolved to the point that there is enough variety to satisfy any drumming requirement...from thin, single-ply heads [the original type plastic heads] to those actually made of the same material used in bulletproof vests! These models include thin, medium and heavy versions of coated and clear heads; those that include sound rings that muffle the head and eliminate ringing and overtones; those that are heavy double-ply; those that have small holes punctured along the outside diameter of the head [another muffling technique to eliminate overtones]; those with extra plastic in the center of the head touted to focus the sound; and even synthetic heads for those who want the type of sound and feel associated with calfskin.

While there are too many different types of drumheads to really list and describe each of them in this chapter, there are some basic generalities that apply to most all of them:

1) The thinner the head, the more overtones [ring] it produces.
2) The heavier [thicker] the head the less overtones produced.
3) Clear heads have more resonance than coated heads.
4) Coated heads, while giving a slight muffling effect to the overall sound, will produce more stick attack.
5) Heavier weight heads will give less overtones but will also give less stick response when struck...and need to be struck harder to produce the volume of a thin or medium thickness head.
6) Thinner weight heads will give more stick response.
7) Muffled heads will generally be less responsive...and need to be struck harder to produce the same volume as a head without muffling.
8) Heavier, thicker heads will be more durable.
9) Thinner heads will be more sensitive.

Medium heads on the top and bottom of the drum will give a well rounded sound while thin heads top and bottom will give a brighter sound and be more responsive. Heavy, double-ply heads on both sides will give a more muffled effect with less response and projection. For this reason, heavier heads are very often used with a thinner, medium weight head on the bottom to give more response and projection.

All drumhead types can be mixed to take advantage of the characteristics of each. Generally, but not necessarily, when this is done the heavier head is put on the batter side. For example, for normal playing, a medium head can be put on the batter side of a drum with a thin head on the bottom, this getting the warmth of the medium head with the resonance of the thin head. Muffled heads with sound rings are most often used with a more resonant non-muffled medium weight head on the bottom of the drum.

CHAPTER 4

DRUMSTICKS, ETC.

Butt End · Practical Balance Point · Shoulder · Neck · Bead or Tip

All drummers are aware of the fact that drumsticks come in all weights, shapes and sizes. The materials range from wood to synthetics. There were even sticks made of steel at one time which were extremely heavy and which drummers used to practice with in the belief they would build wrist strength. That practice has stopped since it was discovered that steel sticks were so heavy they could actually do damage by putting a strain on the muscles, ligaments and joints in the wrist and hand.

Picking a stick is a very personal thing and is sometimes an ongoing process. The search for a stick usually begins by using the make and model endorsed by a famous drummer someone might admire. Some drummers hope that changing their sticks will make them play better or get a different sound. The truth is that the only thing that makes one play better is practice; and the best way to get a good sound is to develop a good "touch". (For example, playing off the drum.)

STICK CHARACTERISTICS

Whatever the size or style of stick used there are a few generalities that apply to all sticks:

1) The bigger the stick the more full the drum sound. This also means that when a large stick is played on a cymbal more cymbal sound will be heard rather than stick sound.

2) The lighter the stick the less rebound. However, the reverse is not <u>necessarily</u> true.

3) The lighter the stick the more stick sound.

4) The more surface contact of the bead with the drumhead the easier it is to play a roll. Example: round beads roll easy.

5) The smaller the bead the more stick sound.

6) The more dense (harder) the stick the more shock felt by the hands.

7) The less dense the stick the more shock is absorbed by the stick, the less is transferred to the hands.

8) The less dense the stick the less rebound and vice-versa.

9) The more dense the stick the longer it should last.

10) Wood sticks with wood tips give a warmer sound on drums and cymbals than synthetic sticks or tips.

Examples of density in wood sticks:

Maple - light weight, low density. Light sound. Less rebound. Light vibration and shock transfer to hands.

Hickory - medium weight and density. Absorb vibrations and shock well. Warm sound on drums and cymbals.

Oak - high density and heavier weight. Clean sound on cymbals, slightly heavier sound than hickory. More shock to hands. Most durable of the three.

BRUSHES

Brushes come in two basic types: wire and nylon (or plastic).

The wire brushes will give a softer, lighter sound. They are great for snare work, which seems logical since playing with wires on the batter head complements the wires on the snare side. However, they have no natural <u>rebound</u> and the wire strands can easily bend out of shape.

The nylon or plastic brushes give a more full and also louder sound. They also rebound much easier than wire brushes and keep their shape much better since the strands will snap back into place when bent.

Both wire and nylon brushes come in light and heavy weights.

MALLETS

Mallets are also called timpani sticks because their origin was that they were developed to play the timpani or "kettle drums" in a symphony orchestra.

Like sticks, mallets come in all different sizes and the heads are made of various materials - usually felt - and come in soft, medium and hard densities.

The soft and medium heads are generally best for drum set work to simulate a "timp" roll, get Latin effects and play cymbal swells. Drum solos with mallets can also be very creative.

Mallets should be an addition to every drummer's arsenal of sticks and brushes.

CHAPTER 5

SMOOTHING OUT THE LONG ROLL

One of the most admirable sounds in all of drumming is a great Long Roll - from the open "machine gun" sound to the closed "sandpaper" sound.

We all know the Long Roll (or double stroke roll) consists of two strokes with each hand - a wrist stroke followed by a rebound or bounce stroke, the wrist stroke being naturally stronger than the rebound stroke. The secret of a smooth Long Roll, is the accenting of the rebound stroke to make it as strong as the wrist stroke.

When written as eighth notes the accented roll would look like this:

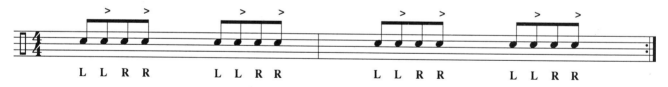

Most drummers struggle with this concept as it feels much more natural to put the accent on the first stroke (wrist) rather than on the second stroke (rebound).

However, there is a successful system to alleviate the difficulty in accenting the rebound stroke. To get a full understanding of this system we will take it in steps.

First of all, play a standard "shuffle" beat with one hand at a time, accenting the 2nd and 4th beats:

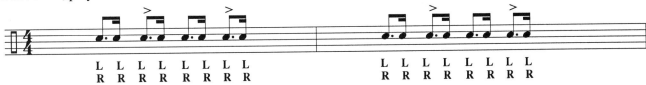

Do the same "shuffle" but now accenting <u>all</u> of the down beats, concentrating on lifting the stick off of the drumhead as quickly as possible after making the accent:

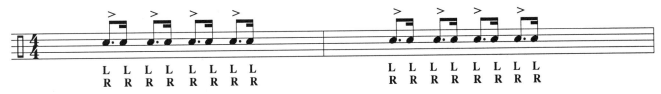

After practicing with each hand individually, alternate the hands for one measure each:

Next, change the rhythm slightly and alternate the hands every two beats:

Finally, we will change the sticking and alternate the hands every beat:

Slowly build the speed on this exercise and as it gets faster the dotted-eighth and sixteenth note pattern will even out and become straight eighth notes:

As you get even faster with this the eighths will naturally become sixteenths, thirty-seconds, etc. and you will be rolling with an accent on the weak or rebound beat. Once you have developed this exercise into a smooth roll it is an easy matter to change to the traditional sticking of RRLL and continue to accent your rebound stroke.

CHAPTER 6

ROLLING IN METER

Whenever rolling for a specific number of beats the drummer should play a specific number of notes. Even when playing the "multiple stroke" roll (aka the "buzz" or "press" roll) the multiple strokes are based on a specific subdivision of the beat.

The accepted note value for rolls in 4/4 time is thirty-second notes. This notation can change, of course, in accordance with time signatures and tempo. But the general roll values per beat are as follows:

As examples, a 5-stroke roll is noted ♪ which is actually played [notation] while a 9-stroke roll is noted ♪ and is played [notation] .

This notation could be described as a music writing shorthand. For instance, ♪ would mean to play thirty-second notes for the duration of an eighth note; ♩ would be thirty-second notes for the duration of a quarter note; ♩ would be thirty-second notes for the duration of a half note; and 𝅝 would be thirty-second notes for the duration of a whole note, etc.

There are times when the tempo is either too fast or too slow for thirty-second notes to fit comfortably within the meter. For a very fast tempo, one solution is to substitute sixteenth note triplets for the thirty-second notes. In doing this, six notes per beat are played instead of eight notes per beat.

Example:

For a very slow tempo, thirty-second note triplets will often fill the space comfortably and in meter.

Example:

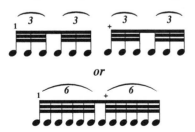

Note that the roll is played in a logical variation of the thirty-second notes (or triplets) of the regular long roll and played "in meter" as opposed to random rolling which is ambiguous to the listener.

Wrong:

Correct:

The stick should not be dug into the drumhead when applying the extra pressure. They should be "buzzed" in an upward motion off the drum.

Tip: This roll can also be played by moving the sticks off the drumhead in a circular motion with the right stick moving clockwise while the left stick moves counter-clockwise.

Another solution to very slow or fast tempi is to use the multiple stroke, "press", or "buzz" roll. This can be used to substitute for a closed double stroke roll at a very fast tempo or to play extra notes at a very slow tempo.

The multiple bounce roll is done by simply adding some extra finger pressure when playing a double stroke roll to achieve more than two strokes per hand. It is usually played at the edge of the drumhead near the rim.

Example:

Multiple Stroke Roll:

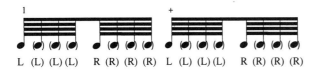

CHAPTER 7

DRUMSET CONCEPTS

The drummer's personal approach to the drumset determines how he or she plays, sounds and feels. This approach takes in many factors from touch and technique to the sizes of the drums and cymbals used, the size of the drumset itself, drumheads, sticks, etc., plus intangibles like how he feels both physically and mentally at that particular time.

The primary concept that affects a drummer's style and sound is how he approaches the drumset. Basically there are two concepts: 1) as a collection of separate instruments (drums, cymbals, etc.) much like a small percussion section; and 2) as the drumset being one complete instrument with different tones, colors, highs, lows, etc.

It has been my experience that the latter is the concept used by the best drummers I have ever heard. Just as a pianist or organist approaches the keyboard and pedals as one complete instrument, so should the drummer approach the drumset.

The drumset is <u>an</u> <u>instrument</u> and should be approached that way. This concept helps the drummer make a smoother transition when moving from one part of the instrument to another.

The second influence on a drummer's sound is his/her touch and technique and this could arguably be considered the primary influence. Ten drummers could play the same snare drum, cymbal or drumset and due to differences in touch, it could feasibly sound like ten different instruments. Great drummers will play someone else's drumset and it will sound like his own set while conversely, someone will sit in on that great drummer's set and it just will not sound the same. Again, touch is a major factor here.

Frequently a student will bring a record or tape to me and say "I want my snare drum to sound like this. How do I do it?" There are many questions involved here: What size is the drum? Is it wood or metal? How many snares? Are they wire? Or gut? What are the drumheads? The sticks? Wood or synthetic? Are the tips wood or nylon? If the stick is wood is it maple, hickory, oak or one of the exotic woods occasionally used? How many microphones were used? Were both heads miked? Were equalization (treble, bass, mid-range) adjustments and/or other effects added by the engineer during recording and/or mixing? Was any muffling used or was the drum wide open?

It is obvious that trying to copy another's drum sound is close to impossible, and even if accomplished, the difference in touch and technique will make it sound different. In addition, when trying to copy anyone else's sound, style, etc., the drummer is losing his own individuality.

This is not to say a drummer should not use someone he respects as a frame of reference or as a level of playing to reach a goal, but it should be remembered that no matter how well done, as in any great art, a copy is still just a copy and will never be as great as the original.

CHAPTER 8

BASS DRUM AND HI-HAT

As with finger systems and hand positions there are many variations of foot technique but these variations are derived from two basic techniques.

The Bass Drum: The first technique is common to both the bass drum and hi-hat and that is simply planting the heel on the heelplate of the pedal and rocking the foot forward so the toes push the pedal down.

With the bass drum this technique is especially good at slow to medium speeds and affords very precise control of placement of the notes. If the beater is not buried and kept pressed against the drumhead after the stroke is made, but released and allowed to return to the starting position, a fairly quick second stroke can be made when more speed is required. By releasing the beater immediately and allowing it to leave the head more tone is extracted from the drum. It is much like playing "off" the drum and "drawing the sound out of the drum" as covered in the very beginning (Chapter 1) of this book.

The second technique for the bass drum is one in which the foot is placed on the pedals and the heel is then raised at the ankle, forcing the ball of the foot and toes downward. This pushes the pedal down and causes the beater to hit the drumhead. Again, if the heel is immediately back down and the beater is released from the drumhead much speed can be obtained by constant repetition of this technique - and even more when used in conjunction with the first technique.

A sliding technique is also possible: when raising the heel to make the stroke, slide the foot forward on the pedal changing the foot angle and leverage and causing the beater to get a double stroke. With practice, triplets and quadruples can easily be obtained.

Tip: Whatever technique is used, the ball of the foot should always be in contact with the pedal footplate.

The Hi-Hat: With the hi-hat the rocking technique works perfectly to open and close the hi-hat cymbals when they are being played with sticks or for an occasional "splash" effect by making the cymbals hit together loosely and allowed to ring. For getting a good "chick" sound from the hi-hat or for playing faster notes and splashes, the second method should be employed.

To begin this technique, place the ball of the foot on the footplate of the hi-hat stand with your heel in the air and holding the cymbals together tightly with the ball of the foot. Next bring the heel down and make it strike the heelplate of the stand and immediately return it to the starting position in the air. Repeat the process counting "1-2-3-4" in succession as the heel touches the heelplate. Be sure and keep the cymbals held tightly together.

Once comfortable with this motion, just before counts "2 and 4", quickly lift the ball of the foot and bring it back down instantly causing the cymbals to open slightly and close again on "2 and 4". This could also be described as a quick "skip" movement on those beats. (As with the bass pedal, the ball of the foot should "ride" the footplate and always be in contact with it.)

When this technique is mastered the drummer not only has the ability to get a great "chick" sound from the hi-hat but will also have a timekeeper in the process since the heel will be moving on all four counts. For odd time signatures simply put the skip motion on the beats where the "chick" is desired.

Tip: Once mastered, make the heel come down <u>almost</u> to the heel plate but not quite striking it. This will prevent any unwanted clicks from the heel contact.

CHAPTER 9

CYMBALS

Although cymbals are instruments in themselves, when used in a drumset they become part of <u>that</u> <u>instrument</u>. Cymbals have characteristics and the choice and use of certain cymbals is as personal a signature a drummer can have.

Merchandising propaganda aside, there are two general types of cymbals: those designated as cast and those designated as hand hammered. All cymbals are cast and hammered to some extent by the amount of hand hammering to achieve a desired type of sound is what influences the designation of the cymbal as cast or hand hammered.

A cymbal designated as cast will have a precise clear sound with controlled overtones. When struck with a stick the sound would be like a "ting". One designated as hand hammered will have a darker sound with more overtones and when struck would have a sound like "tah".

Whatever other designations a cymbal may have (ride, crash, splash, etc.) they are there to describe the additional characteristics of that particular cymbal. For example, a "Ride" cymbal will have few overtones and tend to be thicker than a "Crash" cymbal. This tells the buyer that this "Ride" cymbal will have a clearer stick sound without as many overtones for time-keeping whereas the "Crash" tells the buyer it will react to the stick with a quicker response and more spread to the sound. Remember, however, that one drummer's "Crash" is another drummer's

"Ride" and vice-versa, and that the designations are on the cymbal for description of the sound within the parameters of that particular cymbal company.

General Rules:

1) Heavy cymbals are higher pitched than thin cymbals and build overtones more slowly.

2) Thin cymbals have a lower sound, react and build overtones more quickly, but also decay more quickly.

3) The smaller the bell or cup of the cymbal the less overtones.

4) The greater the arc or curve of a cymbal the more overtones.

5) Flat ride cymbals have no bell and little arc or curve, hence, very few overtones and a clear stick sound.

6) Hi-hat cymbals should be paired with the heavier of the two as the bottom cymbal.

CHAPTER 10

THE GROOVE

The groove, feel, pulse, beat, pocket - whatever it is called - is the essence of the feeling of the music being played. Musical genre has its own concept and texture - almost a personality.

(In classical music the composer is the main force in the music's texture and interpretation. Very specific instructions for the feeling of a piece and dynamic markings are included by the composer to guide the performer's interpretation of the music. Percussion is used mainly as a coloring for the music and as a support for other sections of the orchestra.)

Whatever the feeling or essence of the music being played, it is the drummer's job to help create and maintain the essence. Rhythms, fills and short solos should be played in the context of the music and musical form to maintain the "groove."

FORM

All music is written with definite patterns or sequences of melody, harmony and rhythm. This is called "form" of the music. Even avant-garde or free-form music actually can be considered to have form because once a tonality or rhythm is established that becomes the "A" section of the piece - if it changes to another tone center or rhythm, that would be considered the "B" section and the form would be AB. If it never changes, the form would simply be A - but it would have form even if considered "open" form. If the music has a beginning and an ending it has "form".

The two most common forms of music the drumset player is likely to encounter are the 12-bar blues and 32-bar song forms. The 12-bar blues or some derivative of it is used in all styles of popular music from country to rock to jazz. It is a twelve bar chord progression based on the first, fourth and fifth notes of a diatonic scale. Many people write this chord progression with Roman numerals, and it usually goes like this: I-IV-I-I—IV-IV-I-I—V-IV-I-I. Or, to simplify it somewhat: I (4 bars), IV (2 bars), I (2 bars), V (1 bar), IV (1 bar), I (2 bars). There are different variations of this including the 24-bar blues, but once the 12-bar blues progression is understood all other derivations are easily followed.

The 32-bar song form is very widely used in contemporary music from pop to jazz to Broadway shows and movies. This form is designated A-A-B-A and is formed as follows: an 8 bar phrase of a melody and chord progression (A); the same phrase repeated (A); a completely different phrase (this is called the "bridge" or "release") (B); the original phrase repeated again (A).

There are many different forms. Some examples:

1) Phrase (A); bridge (B); phrase (A) - ABA form

2) 16 bar song form: 8 bar phrase (A); different 8 bar phrase (B) - AB form

3) 8 bar phrase (A); different phrase (B); a third phrase (C); the original phrase (A) - ABCA form

4) Rondo type form: phrase (A); different phrase (B); original phrase (A); another different phrase (C); original phrase (A) - ABACA form

Knowing the form of a piece of music is immensely helpful in making logical sense of the music and following an arrangement of that music. Everything that is played by the drummer must be in correlation to that particular form of the music or it is inappropriate. The drummer <u>must</u> <u>play</u> <u>the</u> <u>tune</u>!

"2" & "4": THE DRUMMER'S BEATS

It was explained to me by a jazz pianist and musicologist why the drummer's hi-hat should have a strong "chick" sound on beats "2" and "4". He said it was one of the elements of swing - the bass played long tones on "1" and "3" and the hi-hat cut them off with a strong "chick" on "2" and "4".

Accenting the second and fourth beats also creates momentum in another way. The tonic chord of a song is the chord of the key signature. For example, a song in the key of C has C for the tonic chord, a song in F has F for the tonic chord, etc. Songs most often begin and end on the tonic chord and these chords generally are played on beats "1" and "3". Therefore, songs <u>most</u> <u>often</u> end on beats "1" and "3". If the drummer is accenting those beats the feeling will be sluggish (like a march) and will also give a possible feeling of finality whenever a tonic chord is played. However, when the drummer accents "2" and "4" momentum is created because it feels like another beat should follow. Songs do not <u>generally</u> end on "2" or "4" so another ("1" or "3") needs to be played. The drummer then answers with another accent on "2" or "4" and a feeling of forward motion is created until the end of the song when everyone ends together.

Hence, the song has a "groove".

SLOW GROOVES

The longer time duration between notes make keeping a slow tempo accurate much more difficult than fast tempi (tempos). The slower the tempo the more difficult it can be.

One method for keeping slow grooves even is to subdivide the beat in your head while playing. For example, four quarter notes at a very slow tempo such as MM ♩ = 44 would normally be counted:

By subdividing to eighth notes, your counting could be:

Or even to sixteenth notes:

This puts less space between the notes in your counting and helps to keep the time accurate.

THE METRONOME

The first job of the drummer is to keep time. Without good time, nothing else will work. You cannot have a great groove unless the time is there first.

The metronome is one of the best ways to develop a musician's time - and contrary to some opinions it will not make your playing stiff, just accurate.

The markings MM on music stands for Mälzel's Metronome. MM ♩ = 120 means to set the metronome at 120 and each tick will represent a quarter note. Actually, that is two beats per second. (A metronome set at 60 ticks is at <u>one</u> beat per second.)

There are many ways to use a metronome, the first being to set the tick at each beat in the measure as described above. Accuracy can then be improved by setting it to tick every other beat and then once a measure. For example, if working on a technique or piece of music in 4/4 time @ MM ♩ = 160, first the metronome would be set at 160, then at 80, then at 40 - but the musician would still continue playing at 160, therefore hearing just one tick per measure and having to rely on his own accuracy rather than a tick on every beat.

The time spent with a metronome is invaluable and the first time a drummer is called on to play along with a "click track" in a recording situation that value will be greatly appreciated.

CHAPTER 11

THE SMALL SET CHALLENGE

Snare, bass, ride cymbal and hi-hat - the four piece drumset. A second cymbal is sometimes added to make it a five piece set. And any drummer who can play - can really play - can do almost any gig on this small set-up. The exception would be shows and big band work where the extra colors of the toms is desirable or a simulated timpani roll is needed.

Most aspiring young drummers look forward to owning a drumset with double bass drums, multiple toms, two snare drums, two hi-hats and an array of cymbals stacked on top of each other surrounding him. Quite a set-up! But when the set is attained, ninety percent of the drummers sound alike. Typical of this sound is the descending tom-tom fill using sixteenth notes:

This tom-tom fill syndrome is easy to fall into as rhythmic creativity suffers.

Jazz, rock, funk, country, Latin, casuals or club dates, etc., can all be played with a small set. And because the drummer is limited in the amount of drums and colors at his disposal, playing a small set encourages the drummer to use his imagination and be creative both rhythmically and melodically.

All beginning drummers should study with the four piece set as described, adding the second cymbal only after full exploration of the four pieces has been accomplished. And the more experienced drummer who never mastered the small set should take the challenge and study it also. It will open up brand new avenues never before traveled - and will be easier to carry around and quicker to set-up and tear down.

CHAPTER 12

THE DRUM RUDIMENTS

While opinions differ on the study of the drum rudiments it is generally agreed to that the <u>basic</u> rudiments should be studied and mastered by all drummers. In addition, most educators and professionals believe that the serious percussionist should have a knowledge of and attain at least a certain proficiency in all forty drum rudiments. The controversy arises on the degree of importance of the rudiments and the <u>method</u> of studying them.

The traditional method for learning and practicing the rudiments, open to closed to open, is a proven method for developing hand speed and coordination and also good training for music that requires an accelerando. However, it is believed by many that this method of practice is conducive to subconsciously learning to speed up the tempo when executing "breaks" and "fills" while playing with other musicians.

To help prevent this problem I believe the rudiments should be practiced using two additional methods <u>along</u> <u>with</u> the proven traditional method of open to closed. First, the rudiments should be practiced at different <u>steady</u> tempi, preferably with a metronome, stopping completely before increasing the speed. (I'm a firm believer in the value of the metronome not only for developing steady time and note duration awareness but also in preparation for studio work using a "click" track.)

Secondly, they should be practiced increasing the tempo by doubling exactly the beginning tempo. For example, single or double strokes would be played as quarter notes for a period of time, doubling to eighth notes, doubling again to sixteenth notes, etc., then reversing the process back to the original quarter notes.

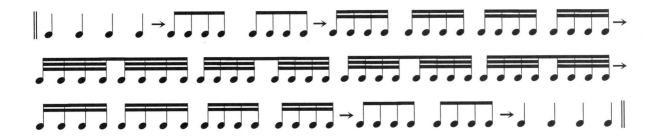

This develops the hands while at the same time give an awareness of time, note values and sub-division. Naturally, the beginning tempo of the quarter notes should be varied to cover the full spectrum of time possibilities.

CHAPTER 13

THE JAZZ INSTRUMENT

The drumset is the <u>only</u> instrument that was specifically created to play jazz. Consequently, every drumset player should learn at least <u>some</u> jazz concepts and techniques. This is why the instrument was developed and it should be explored to gain a fuller meaning of its tradition. There is a saying: "You have to go back before you can go forward". That simply means one must learn the basics, tradition, etc. of what he is doing before the ability is acquired to develop something new. Learning the tradition makes what it experimented with in the future, stronger and valid.

The basis for any type of jazz is "swing" - and the drummer swings by playing the jazz cymbal "ride". This "ride" is the continuous beat which is kept on the cymbal and is central to the jazz drummer's support of the other musicians in the band.

Some musicians insist that the actual cymbal ride cannot be written and that it is a "feeling" that has to be learned. Others have tried to write it as closely as possible by dividing the beat into odd groupings of notes and rests. It has even been written by musicologists as combinations of quarter notes and quintuplets.

All these seem to be moot points anyway because throughout the history of jazz drumming different drummers have played the ride rhythm different ways.

The jazz ride is normally written as a quarter note, dotted-eighth note and sixteenth note:

And it is sometimes written as a quarter note and eighth note triplet combination:

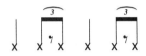

However, it is generally accepted that whichever way the ride is written, it is interpreted in the triplet form. This should be practiced and learned precisely and then can be used as a point of departure as the drummer's own individual approach to the cymbal ride is expressed.

It is important in traditional "swing" music for the drummer to accent the 2nd and 4th beats of each measure in 4/4 time. This is accomplished by adding the hi-hat on those beats along with the cymbal ride. It is an element of "swing" that the hi-hat plays against the "one" and "three" of the bass player; and accenting "two" and "four" gives a feeling of momentum to the music because it is contrary to the beats where the tonic chords normally fall and songs normally end.

Now we have the cymbal ride and hi-hat and the rhythm looks like this:

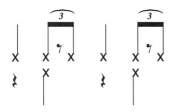

In older styles the bass drum was played on "one" and "three" or all four beats. However, in modern forms from bebop on, though the bass drum is still often played on all four beats (this is referred to as "four on the floor") it is just as often used mainly for accents ("dropping bombs") and improvising. An example of both styles is big band drumming where a light four to the beat pulse on the bass drum ("feathering") is desirable because it adds more "bottom" to the sound of the band.

The snare drum and tom-toms are also generally used for accents and improvising excepts when specific rhythms are played in a jazz context in which a steady pulse is required. These could be anything from a backbeat on "two" and "four" to a march to a Latin rhythm with a definite clave (rhythm pattern) such as a bossa nova.

In very progressive "hip" jazz styles (eg: avant-garde) the timekeeping is no longer kept solely with the ride cymbal and hi-hat but with the whole drumset as a unit. The basic feeling is kept but is also improvised.

Example:

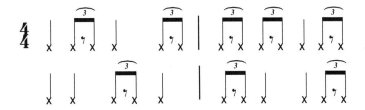

An example of timekeeping using the complete drumset would be:

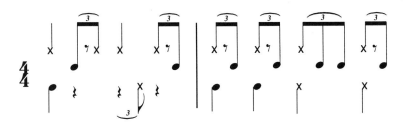

Improvisation is a strong element of jazz and is also coordinated within the jazz ride pulse - or as a counterpoint to it.

Whatever the rhythm patterns played and how they are broken up, the pulse of 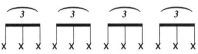 should continue to fit into the framework of the time feeling.

As final examples, the jazz ride could be written in cut-time (2/2) and played on the hi-hat. This creates a half-time feel which can be adapted to rock, funk or hip-hop.

Example:

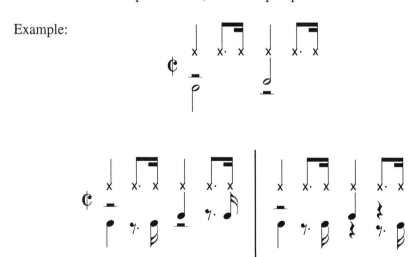

CHAPTER 14

PRACTICE

There is a saying regarding practicing that has been attributed to the concert pianist Vladimir Horowitz and paraphrased by many. One version of this saying is: "If I miss one day I know it. If I miss two days my wife knows it. If I miss three days my audience knows it." That is arguably the consummate statement on the importance of regular practice.

Time spent practicing brings up the old debate of quality versus quantity. If the musician's focus is right, more can be accomplished in thirty minutes time than two hours of time with the instrument.

Many musicians do not really practice but "play" their instruments. That is to say that they sit down (or stand) with the instrument and play what they know. This can be great for the maintenance or polishing of certain techniques but, with those exceptions, no progress is being made.

The essence of the practice session should be musicality while striving for perfection and improvement. Even while practicing, the musician should concentrate on <u>playing music</u>!

Perfection, improvement and musicality are the guidelines for a productive practice session.

Perfection: Every technique should be done as perfectly as possible. This includes hand positions, stickings, stick height, wrist movements, touch, etc. Practicing wrong will develop improper technique - and all execution is affected by technique. To strive for perfection is the first step in practicing.

Improvement: Each practice session should create a challenge for the musician to accomplish something never previously done. This could be a new rudiment, piece of music, or exercise. It could also be a new tempo for an old exercise, etc. And the tempo does not necessarily have to be faster - just different. Old exercise books are excellent ways to improve. (Every book should be played at least twice, because it is never mastered the first time through.) But, whatever it is, some new accomplishment should be attempted at every practice session.

Musicality: The purpose of playing any instrument is to play music. And the music should be kept foremost in mind whenever practicing. Even when playing a rudiment or technical exercise it should be thought of musically and how it can be applied to music. As stated earlier, musicality is the essence of playing an instrument.

The amount of practice time will vary from individual to individual and also from beginner to professional. A beginning drummer might practice thirty minutes to one hour a day and increase that to two hours per day as he progresses after the first year or so of study. If the student continues to be serious and is looking toward or is in a college program as a music major, the practice time should increase to approximately two or four hours per day. As a struggling career minded professional it can increase to four to eight hours per day. As steady engagements, playing situations and other responsibilities increase with a developing career (and with life in general) practice time then starts to decrease again. It might be one to two hours per day again or maybe two to four hours three times a week - whatever the individual needs are and professional and personal schedule allow. But, whatever the situation allows, practice should be continued throughout one's professional life under any conditions.

Modern medicine now has practitioners who specialize in problems peculiar to musicians of all instruments. Two problems for drummers are carpal tunnel syndrome and lower back pain. To alleviate and/or prevent some of these problems experts recommend resting for five minutes each half hour instead of continuous practice. The recommendation is twenty five minutes - practice, five minutes - rest.

If possible, the practice session should include specific individual problems but also cover the gamut rather than isolating one particular phase of drumming - or different coverage could be done on different days.

1) Daily:

   1/4 technique; 1/4 reading; 1/4 independence or new rhythms; 1/4 playing/creating.

2) Weekly:

Monday	Technique, reading, playing/creating.
Tuesday	Technique, independence, playing/creating.
Wednesday	Rhythms, reading, playing/creating.
Thursday	Technique, independence, playing/creating.
Friday	Reading, technique, playing/creating.
Saturday	Technique, independence, playing/creating.
Sunday	Rest or just play.

Note that these are just suggestions of a guideline for the individual to adapt to his/her needs. Also note that "technique" includes hands or feet and the rudiments.

Finally, "playing/creating" was included every day because it is very important to do what we are striving for as much as possible - play the drums and enjoy them. But this time period could very well be used to also work on fills and solo ideas - but playing musically!

12 TIPS TO EFFECTIVE PRACTICING

The hours we all put into practicing technique are very important to us. We all do it to maintain or improve our playing. However, often much of the time spent behind the drums is not put to the best use.

For this reason I have made a list of some important points that if adhered to should not only make your practice session more productive but also more enjoyable. (We all enjoy what we're doing much more when we can see advancement and improvement.) Some of these points have been covered in previous chapters but I have included them again because of their importance:

1) Watch Your Hand Position: this is the No. 1 problem I have found with students - from beginner to advanced. Always be sure your hands are in the correct position. It just doesn't make sense to put time in practicing technique and not have your hand positions correct. These positions are used for a reason and your development will be limited if you do not use them correctly. Once your hand position improves you will find your playing will become much cleaner and faster.

2) Sticking: this is the second biggest problem I've come across in teaching. Keep in mind the phrase "one stick up, one stick down" and practice that way. You will always have a stick in position to make a stroke either from the high ("up") position or from the low ("down") position. With concentration on "sticking" your hand techniques will start to flow much more smoothly.

3) Stick Height: this is different from sticking in that it refers to how high you bring the sticks. Whether you work from a full 90 degree position, a 45 degree angle or anything in between the important point is that both sticks return to the same height. Because most of us are not ambidextrous we have a tendency to favor our strong hand and bring that stick to a higher position than the weak hand. This means one stick is traveling a shorter distance to reach the drum whenever a stroke is made. Think about it. It stands to reason that if one stick is traveling eight inches and the other only five inches, the stick farther away has to move faster to reach the drum in the same time interval as the closer stick. This also means the rebounds will be weaker with the closer stick. Are your Single Strokes and Long Rolls uneven? Stick height is probably at least part of the reason - along with the Hand Position and Sticking. Concentrate on these three common problems and you will see a vast improvement in your technique.

4) Play Off The Drum: unless they have learned this somewhere along the way, most drummers, especially heavy hitters, play down into the drum instead of off it. When making your stroke think up and bring the stick away from the head immediately after striking it. Some teachers describe this as "drawing" or "pulling" the sound out of the drum. The shorter the time the stick is on the drumhead the more resonant and responsive the drum will be. Thus, a cleaner and fuller tone and increased stick speed.

5) Learn And Practice The Rudiments: even if you only spend a minimal amount of time on them do at least something. If you only study one rudiment a week - just one - you will have learned all 40 in less than ten months. You do not have to be a rudimental champ but the knowledge will be definite plus - and you'll feel good about your accomplishment besides.

6) Work With A Metronome: use it at different speeds including the slowest ones. It won't make your playing stiff but will improve your time and meter. And, if you ever encounter a click track in the recording studio you will be thankful for any time spent with a metronome.

7) Practice Every Day: at least something. We all know that occasionally time is at a premium and a full practice session is impossible. On those days at least do something - even if it's just a 10 or 15 minute warm-up routine. Keep the practicing habit!

8) Strive For Perfection: be as perfect as possible when practicing. There is no sense in putting in the time and hard work if you don't go for perfection. Be your own worst toughest critic and don't sell yourself short.

9) Vary Your Practice Routine: this is especially helpful when practice time is limited. Sometimes it is better to look at your practice sessions on a weekly instead of daily basis. One day spend the majority of the time on hands another on independence, another on reading, another on rudiments, etc. and be sure to rest for a few minutes between segments or five minutes per half hour. This will help avoid overuse or strain of your muscles. Be sure and spend some time creating and just playing. Some teachers suggest you do it at the end of your

practice session. However, I have found it often works better to do it at the very beginning to get it out of your system. Then you can just focus on what you planned to work on that day.

10) In Regard To Sticks: you should generally use the same size stick to practice with that you play with. But it can be beneficial to spend a few minutes a week with heavier or lighter sticks to give your hand and wrist muscles a change. This can improve strength and reflexes.

11) Study The Traditional Grip: and if you generally play traditional spend some time playing matched. The traditional grip has some definite advantages which include finger dexterity and flexibility of the weak hand. If you generally play matched grip, spend at least <u>some</u> time every day on the traditional grip. The increase in finger dexterity will even help your matched grip playing.

12) Keep Challenging Yourself: never be satisfied. Try to be working on something new at all times - a rudiment, book, rhythm - and once that is accomplished, whether it takes a day, a week or a month, move on to something else new. Strive to constantly improve during each practice session.

These previous tips should be concentrated on only while practicing. Once you are at rehearsals or the gig don't think about them. Concentrate on the music and feeling relaxed and comfortable. If you use these tips diligently every time you practice you will find they will creep into your playing without your realizing it and you will see a vast improvement in your technique and playing in a few short months.

CHAPTER 15

Warm-Ups

SYNOPSIS

This is a 15 exercise snare drum workout that contains a variety of essentials: single and double strokes, duple and triple meter, rolls, accents and rudiments. It contains the seven essential drum rudiments as recommended by the Percussive Arts Society and can be used as a quick warm-up using just a practice pad to work the hands, or can be expanded into a serious practice session using a full set of drums working between the hands and feet. It should be practiced as is and then used as a guideline for adaptation to each drummer's individual needs.

INTRODUCTION

I'm a firm believer in both regular practice (whatever level player you are) and warming up before a gig or performance Some musicians feel that warming up is unnecessary, but that is totally wrong. Musical instruments and especially percussion instruments, are very physical and a certain looseness and flexibility are required to perform on them at optimum efficiency. Warming up properly also helps prevent injuries that are common to musicians in general and drummers in particular. No serious athlete would go into a competition totally cold and no musician should play a gig that way either. It's a great feeling to play smoothly and relaxed because you're properly warmed-up.

The idea that you can be warmed-up by the third or fourth tune doesn't make sense either. Why wait until then to have total command of your instrument? There could be an agent, concert promoter, record company exec. or other important musicians in the audience. They could be there for only one or two tunes and would judge your playing by whatever impression they get in that short time. Besides, sometimes you can even save a train wreck from happening

Daily practice, of course, will keep you in peak form and lessen the need and shorten the time necessary to get warmed-up. However, often due to work, family, etc., regular practice time can be difficult to squeeze into a day. Most of the finest musicians I have ever been in contact with deal with those situations by at least warming-up their chops in some way.

The following routine is just such a warm-up (approximately one to two minutes per exercise) or it can be expanded into a serious practice session. It contains a variety of essentials single and double strokes, duple and triple meter, rolls, accents and rudiments. It can be done using just a pad to work the hands or on a full set of drums working between the hands and feet. Try it as is and then use it as a guideline and adapt it to your own needs.

1) Singles to Doubles (4 times each): I have found this to be one of the best exercises for loosening up. Keep the double strokes high and open.

A ⎪ R L R L RRLLRRLL ⎪ B R L R L RRLLRRLL

C R L R L RRLLRRLL

D R L R L RRLLRRLL

2) Triplets to Doubles (4 times each): Just a variation on number 1 but with more notes per measure. Again, keep all double strokes open.

3) Stroke Rolls (2 times): More rolls but a little tighter and changing meter.

3) Stroke Rolls: Alternate meter changes (2 times).

59

4) Flams and Flam Taps (8 times): Notice the flams are both alternating and non-alternating.

L R ᴸR R L L R R L   L R ᴸR ᴸR ᴸR   R L ʀL ʀL ʀL   L R R ʀL L L ʟR R ʀL L

5) Multiple Rebounds (8-10 times): This exercise is designed mainly for finger practice, especially when doing the triplets and 16ths.

R   L   R   L   R R L L R R L L   R R R L L L R R R L L L   R R R R L L L L R R R R L L L L

6) Paradiddle Inversions (4-8 times): This is great for sticking and concentration. Once you have it down you might want to add the accent for each paradiddle.

R L R R L R L L R L R R L R L L   R L L R L R R L R L L R L R R L

R R L R L L R L R R L R L L R L   R L R L L R L R R L R L L R L R

7) Nonalternating Rudiment: This is an idea giving to me by Danny Pucillo, Sr. The concept is to repeat rudiments with the same hand before alternating. Danny showed to me using the paradiddle, which I have used as the example, but any rudiment will work. Also, alternate rudiments that normally do not alternate, for example the 7-stroke roll.

8) Short Single-Stroke Rolls – also called Single-Stroke Ruffs (4-8 times): This is a variation on what my first drum teacher, Dick Howard, called "spurts." This helped me build my single-stroke roll.

One day do 4's, 5's, 7's and 9's, and another day do 4's, 6's, 8's and 10's.

9) Triplets with Accents (8 times): Alternate between right-hand and left-hand leads. Also, vary the accents with your own ideas.

R L R L R L R L R L R L   etc.

L R L R L R L R L R L R   etc.

10) Mixed Groupings (4 times): Again, alternate right and left leads.

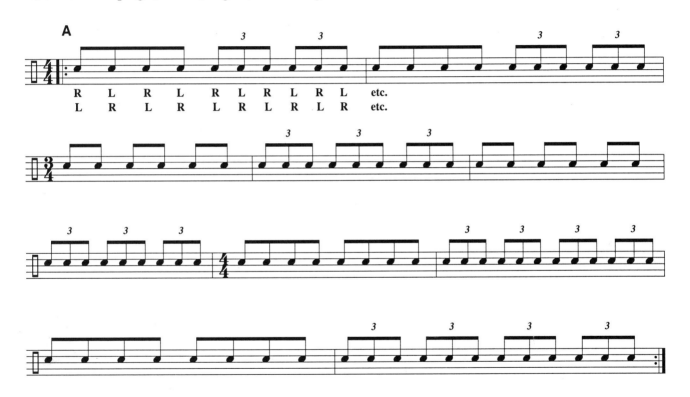

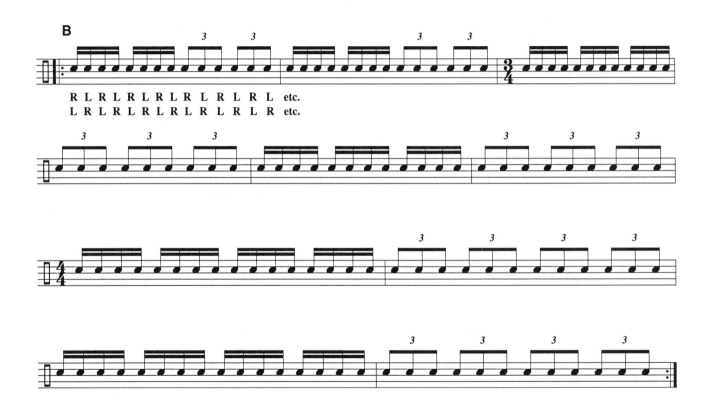

B

R L R L R L R L R L R L R L etc.
L R L R L R L R L R L R L R etc.

11) Accented Long Rolls (8 times): Both normal and alternate sticking.

A

R   R   L   L   R   R   L   L   etc.

B

L   R   R   L   L   R   R   L   etc.

R   L   L   R   R   L   L   R   etc.

12) The Paratriple (8 times): This is a variation of the paradiddle, which presents more of a challange. The same idea can be used with any rudiment that has double strokes by substituting triple strokes.

L R L L L R L R R R L R L L L R L R R R

5-Stroke Rolls (8 times)

R R L L R L L R R L R R R L L L R L L L R R R L

The Drag (8 times)

L L R R R L L L R R R L L L L R R R R L L L L R R R R L

13) Triplets with Mixed Sticking (4-8 times): Start with these stickings and then vary the routine by inventing your own sticking combination.

A
R L L R L L R L L R L L

B
L R R L R R L R R L R R

C
L L R L L R L L R L L R

D
R R L R R L R R L R R L

E
R L L R L L R L L R L L R R L R R L R R L R R L

F
L R R L R R L R R L R R L L R L L R L L R L L R

69

14) Drags or Ruffs (8 times): Alternating and non-alternating.

LLR   RRL   LLR   RRL   LLR   LLR   LLR   LLR   RRL RRL RRL RRL

15) Open to Press Rolls (4-8 times): I saved this for last because it can really tire your hands out fast. Use only extra finger pressure for the press or "buzz" rolls.

open   press

ABOUT MAT MARUCCI

Mat Marucci is an active performer, author, educator, and clinician listed in Who's Who In America and International Who's Who In Music (Cambridge, England). His performing credits include, among others, jazz greats Jimmy Smith, Kenny Burrell, James Moody, Eddie Harris, Buddy De Franco, Les McCann, Pharoah Sanders, and John Tchicai. He also has eight critically acclaimed recordings to his credit as a leader and others as a sideman, including those with John Tchicai and Jimmy Smith, with many of them garnering four stars in various trade magazines including *Jazz Times, Jazziz, and Downbeat.* Mat is the author of several books on drumming for both Lewis Music and Mel Bay Publications, is a faculty member of The JazzSchool (Berkeley, CA), a member of the adjunct faculty for the Los Rios Community College District, an Applied Music instructor for American River College (Sacramento, CA), and an endorser for Mapex drums, Zildjian cymbals, Pro-Mark drumsticks and Remo drumheads. He has also written numerous articles on drumming for *Modern Drummer* magazine, *Downbeat* magazine, the Percussive Arts Society's *Percussion News* and *Percussive Notes* and Pro-Mark's *Upstrokes.* A complete resume can be found at: www.geocities.com/matmarucci/

Mat Marucci uses and endorses:
Mapex drums, Pro-Mark drumsticks
Zildjian cymbals, and Remo drumheads exclusively.

Mat Marucci's Drumset

Zildjian Cymbals
14" New Beat or K Hi-Hats
18" K Constantinople Crash
16" K Dark Crash
20" K Constantinople Ride (Thin-High)
18" K Crash/Ride

Sticks
ProMark Mat Marucci Signature
Stick (Hickory) Model TX927W

Mapex Drums
5¹/₂x14 Maple Snare or
3¹/₂x14 Brass Snare
2 - 8x12 Mounted Toms
14x14 Floor Tom
14x18 Bass Drum

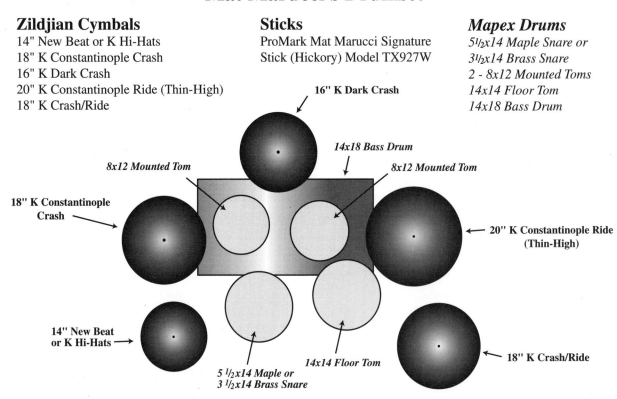

16" K Dark Crash

8x12 Mounted Tom

14x18 Bass Drum

8x12 Mounted Tom

18" K Constantinople Crash

20" K Constantinople Ride (Thin-High)

14" New Beat or K Hi-Hats

5 ¹/₂x14 Maple or 3 ¹/₂x14 Brass Snare

14x14 Floor Tom

18" K Crash/Ride